Behind The Gate

OTHER TITLES BY LESLIE McDONALD

Horse on the Loose

Journeys with Horses

Musings of a Horse Farm Corgi

Down the Aisle

Making Magic

Tic-Tac

Behind The Gate

Leslie McDonald

DOWN THE AISLE PROMOTIONS

Photographs by Leslie McDonald,
Cover Photo by Doug Froh
Art Direction by Morgane Leoni

Contact: www.fcfarm.com or fcfarm@aol.com

ISBN 979-8-9911333-0-2

"Behind the Gate" is dedicated to my husband, Doug, who has shared and supported me through all the challenges, joys and rewards of Full Cry Farm. Thank you for always standing by me.

Contents

Prologue

Rising out of the rows of a southern Ohio cornfield, Full Cry Farm is a childhood dream come to fruition. It was lovingly designed in poetic symmetry with nature to cater to all things equine. Life "behind the gate" flows with the easy rhythm of the seasons, providing a welcoming haven for kindred spirits in search of peace, harmony and a love of horses.

Spring

Cherished childhood dreams

captured in a blossom frame

grow deep roots with age

Guided by birdsong

on a morning walkabout

down a quiet lane

Gaze through concrete eyes
on long ago memories
left beyond the barn

Sprinkled white petals

waiting to be discovered

on a shoreline stroll

A visitor peaks
from hideaway's safe haven
watching who's watching

Pastel loosestrife spikes
stretch toward the sun's halo
draw it back to earth

Whispers of dawn light
stroke the dew from cool spring grass
beckoning morning

Forewarned by thunder

illuminated updraft

swells on horizon

Colors paint the sky
highlighting the chosen path
where wishes await

Summer

Dawn rises above
soft pasture mist awaiting
the touch of hoofprints

Aging garden crane

weathered by the elements

roosts amongst lilies

Rusted garden grace
amongst pale faded petals
embraces July

Garden visitor
munches a succulent treat
of summer bounty

Unfurled sun petals

golden aphrodisiac

enlaced in scarlet

Awake solstice bloom
radiating pastel spikes
to welcome day's dawn

Cold forged steel petals
sprout amongst blushing roses
through lemon grasses

Fresh dew dipped petals
unfurl in summer garden
earthy velvet scent

Lightly settle on

pink blush of August blooms to

sip summer nectar

Bold feathered flyer
perches atop sunflowers
casting season's gold

Fall

Between oaken boards

childhood dreams are realized

pastures of promise

Rusted autumn boughs
stretch toward the pasture fence
shedding crumpled leaves

Arise through sedum
scented blush toned petals wait
for morn to unfurl

Camouflaged amongst
white petaled stalks of primrose
wings outstretched to soar

Looking through pricked ears
foretells the future's promise
framed in remembrance

Petals awaken
caressed from sleep by sunlight
to herald the morn

A feathered flyer

dips his beak to sweet nectar

shadowed 'neath branches

59

Rise from the lilies

homage to partners long passed

ever remembered

Monet's loose brush strokes
paint the sky with florid flames
on azure canvas

Woven morning web

captures autumn images

between silken strands

Winter

Frosted sculpted sky

accentuates frozen prints

breaking the surface

Capping the season
cat tails cast upward fingers
frayed fuzzy tribute

Feedbox furry friends
stare intently down the aisle
awaiting a treat

Beckoned by moon glow
illuminating the path's
eventide secrets

A soul released to

a single cloud in clear sky

heals a heart that mourns

Frozen brass sentries
proudly restrain winter's chill
on December morn

Dreams rise from the mist
on the back of a chestnut
poised to enrapture

Author

Leslie McDonald is an award-winning poet and novelist. She grew up in Chicago and graduated from DePauw University. A Grand Prix level dressage trainer with over 50 professional years in the industry, she lives at Full Cry Farm in southern Ohio where she happily teaches riding lessons and writes books about the special people and animals who bless her life.

Visit **www.fcfarm.com** for more information and to connect with Leslie.